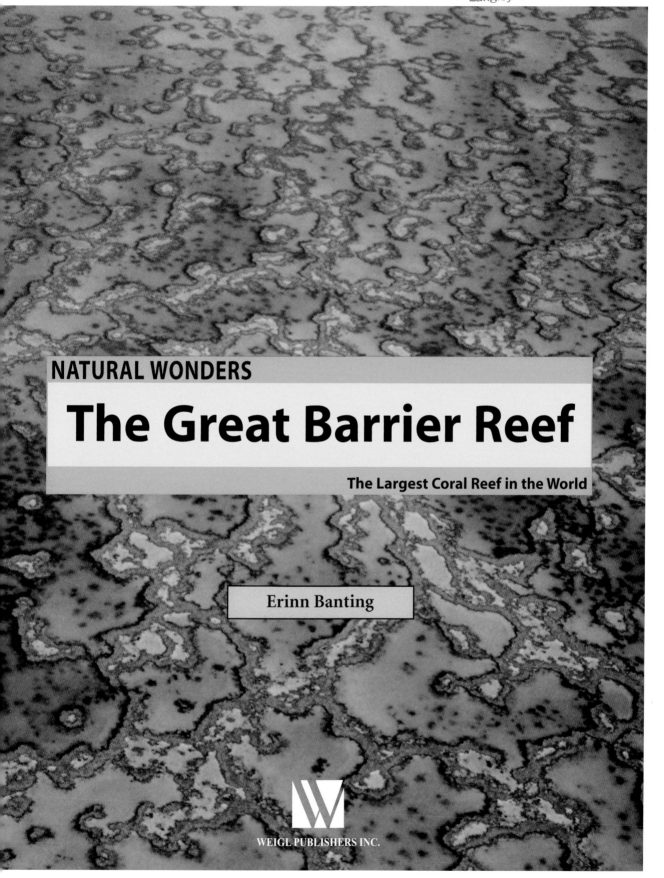

NATURAL WONDERS

The Great Barrier Reef

The Largest Coral Reef in the World

Erinn Banting

WEIGL PUBLISHERS INC.

Published by Weigl Publishers Inc.
350 5th Avenue, Suite 3304, PMB 6G
New York, NY 10118-0069
USA

Web site: www.weigl.com

Library of Congress Cataloging-in-Publication Data

Banting, Erinn.
 The Great Barrier Reef / Erinn Banting.
    p. cm. — (Natural wonders)
 Includes index.
 ISBN 1-59036-272-1 (lib. bdg. : alk. paper) 1-59036-278-0 (pbk.)
 1. Great Barrier Reef (Qld.)—Juvenile literature. 2. Coral reef ecology—
 Australia—Great Barrier Reef (Qld.)—Juvenile literature. I. Title.
 II. Natural wonders (Weigl Publishers)
 GB468.89.B36 2004
 919.43—dc22
                            2004013628
Printed in the United States of America
1 2 3 4 5 6 7 8 9 0   08 07 06 05 04

Editorial Services
BookMark Publishing, Inc.

Editor
Heather C. Hudak

Design
Terry Paulhus

Layout
Biner Design

Photo Researcher
Dawn Friedman,
BookMark Publishing, Inc.

Photo Description
Cover: Reef corals grow close to the sea surface in shallow water that is warmed by sunlight.
Title page: Countless different coral reefs are linked together to form the Great Barrier Reef.

Photograph Credits

Every reasonable effort has been made to trace ownership and to obtain permission to reprint copyright material. The publishers would be pleased to have any errors or omissions brought to their attention so that they may be corrected in subsequent printings.

Cover: The Great Barrier Reef (Dave Fleetham/Tom Stack & Associates); **Copyright Australian Tourist Commission:** page 23; **CORBIS/MAGMA:** pages 1 (Royalty Free), 20 (Penny Tweedie), 24 (Roger Garwood & Trish Ainslie), 27 (Royalty Free); **Corel Corporation:** page 26B; **The Granger Collection, New York:** page 15; **Great Barrier Reef Marine Park Authority:** pages 8, 10, 19, 22, 25R; **Wolfgang Kaehler 2004, www.wkaehlerphoto.com:** page 4; **North Wind Picture Archives:** page 14; **Photo Researchers, Inc.:** page 18 (Tom Hollyman), 25L (Peter Skinner), 26TL (A. Flowers & L. Newman); **Photos.com:** pages 13, 26TR, 28; **Tom Stack & Associates:** pages 6 (Peter Mead), 11 (Dave Fleetham), 12 (Mike Severns); **Tourism Queensland:** page 21 (Peter Lik).

All of the Internet URLs given in the book were valid at the time of publication. However, due to the dynamic nature of the Internet, some addresses may have changed, or sites may have ceased to exist since publication. While the author and publisher regret any inconvenience this may cause readers, no responsibility for any such changes can be accepted by either the author or the publisher.

Contents

The Wonder Down Under

The spectacular Great Barrier Reef is the largest coral reef in the world. It is located off the coast of Australia, one of the most southerly continents on Earth. Australia is so far south of the equator that people call it "down under."

The Great Barrier Reef is not only beautiful, it is also an important **ecosystem.** Scientists study the reef to learn how its many animals live and interact with their environment. Fishers rely on the reef to provide fish for them to catch in nearby waters. Tourists visit the reef to scuba dive and learn about nature.

◼ The wonders of the reef lie very close to the water's surface.

Great Barrier Reef Facts

- The Great Barrier Reef stretches about 1,250 miles (2,012 kilometers) along Australia's northeast coast.

- The Great Barrier Reef is the largest structure in the world built by living organisms.

- There are more than 10,000 different **species** of animals living in the Great Barrier Reef. Some have never been named by scientists.

- The Great Barrier Reef is considered one of the Seven Wonders of the Natural World. Uluru, a huge rock formation, is another Australian site on the list.

- In 1975, the Australian government established the Great Barrier Reef Marine Park to protect the coral reef and its surrounding waters. The huge park covers about 134,000 square miles (347,058 sq km).

Great Barrier Reef Locator

Where in the World?

The Great Barrier Reef lies in a southern portion of the Pacific Ocean called the Coral Sea. The reef begins in the Torres Strait, a narrow body of water that separates northern Australia from Papua New Guinea. From the Torres Strait, the Great Barrier Reef runs south along nearly half of Australia's east coast.

On a map, the Great Barrier Reef looks like a long, underwater wall that separates Australia from the sea. The reef, however, is not a solid wall. It is made up of about 3,000 small reefs and coral islands called cays.

■ **Lady Musgrave Island is a cay, an above-water coral island. Many other underwater coral reefs surround it.**

Puzzler

The Great Barrier Reef is located in the Pacific Ocean, one of the major oceans of the world.

Q What are some of the major oceans of the world?

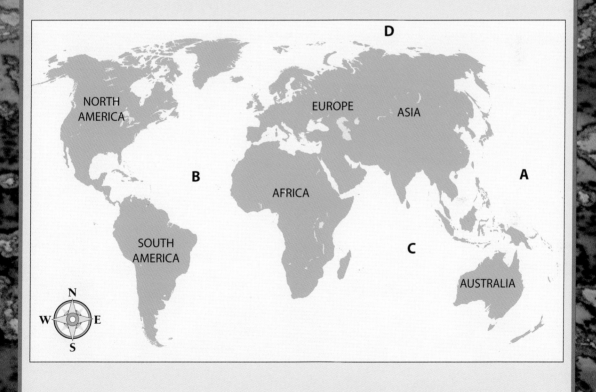

A. Pacific Ocean   B. Atlantic Ocean
C. Indian Ocean   D. Arctic Ocean

A Trip Back in Time

The sea floor on which the Great Barrier Reef sits was formed about 500,000 years ago. Today's reef, however, is very different in size and shape. Coral lives on top of many layers of dead coral from centuries ago.

Coral **polyps** start the process of reef building. These tiny creatures attach themselves to coral rock or other hard surfaces underwater. Polyps become coral as they grow hard skeletons outside their bodies. When certain kinds of coral die, their skeleton shell remains. A reef consists of many of these dead, rocky corals connected to each other. As new polyps grow on dead coral, the life cycle starts over.

Coral polyps are living animals that stay in one place for their entire lives.

Different Kinds of Reefs

Not all coral reefs grow in the same way. These are the three main kinds of reefs. The orange areas represent coral reef.

Side View	Overhead View	Type
		**Fringe reefs** grow in very shallow water surrounding land, such as coasts or islands. These are the youngest types of reefs.
		Barrier reefs grow in deeper water a bit farther offshore. They form a wall, or barrier, between the sea and the shore. A lagoon sits between the reef and shore.
		Atolls are ringed reefs that form away from shore. Some atolls grow around the rim of a sunken volcano.

The Coral Reef Ecosystem

Living communities in nature are called ecosystems. Animals, plants, and the surrounding environment all contribute to making an ecosystem work. Members of ecosystems are divided into groups called producers, consumers, and decomposers. Each of these groups depends on the others for survival.

In the Great Barrier Reef, producers are creatures such as **algae**, that are eaten by consumers. Coral polyps are consumers, feeding off the algae that grow nearby. Thousands of types of fish are also coral reef consumers. Decomposers, such as **bacteria**, are creatures that clean the reef. They eat the waste materials that other animals and plants leave behind.

■ **The sea cucumber is not a vegetable. It is an animal and a decomposer. The sea cucumber crawls along the reef floor, eating waste material.**

Coral Threat

The crown-of-thorns starfish is a dangerous member of the Great Barrier Reef community. Since 1965, scientists have observed periods when the crown-of-thorns population suddenly increased in the reef. This type of starfish is a **predator** of coral. It feeds directly on live coral polyps. So, when the crown-of-thorns population increases, it kills off far too much coral and threatens the entire reef ecosystem.

■ It is difficult for humans to remove the crown-of-thorns starfish from the reef. The dangerous creature is covered with poisonous spines.

Life in the Reef

Some of the most unique and beautiful creatures in the world live in the Great Barrier Reef. Clown, parrot, mandarin, and thousands of other types of fish dart through the coral looking for food and shelter. Larger animals, such as sharks and whales, live nearby. Crabs and sea turtles live in the reef waters, but they sometimes leave the water and crawl around on the beaches.

Many Great Barrier Reef beaches are home to hundreds of bird species, including sandpipers, herons, and terns. These birds are also part of the coral reef ecosystem, as they eat fish from the water. Many birds are just visitors to the area. They **migrate** to Australia every winter from colder countries in the north.

■ **The blue-ringed octopus is one of the reef's deadliest creatures. If bitten by this octopus, an adult human could die after only a few minutes.**

Coral Character

More than 350 different species of coral live in the Great Barrier Reef. They take on many different shapes and colors. Only stony corals grow skeletons outside their bodies and become reefs when they die. Other corals, such as gorgonian coral, grow spines inside their bodies. They do not turn into coral reefs.

The color in coral comes from the algae they eat. Only living corals have color. Dead coral turns white. Coral "bleaching" is a term scientists use when large amounts of coral die and turn white. Bleaching is usually caused by a drastic change in the reef environment. In 1998, sea temperatures around the world increased suddenly, and coral bleaching destroyed large parts of reefs in Australia and other parts of the world.

A certain species of stony coral is called "brain coral."

Early Explorers

The first people to discover the Great Barrier Reef were the **Aboriginal Australians**, who arrived in Australia about 50,000 years ago. Aboriginal groups lived mostly on the coast of Australia and islands of the reef.

Explorers from Asia and Europe visited Australia's shores between the 1300s and 1700s. These visitors did not settle in Australia because the land was hard to farm and was far away from their home countries. When English explorer James Cook sailed to Australia in 1770, he claimed the land for England.

When Captain James Cook arrived in Australia, he named it New South Wales. It reminded him of a part of Great Britain called Wales.

Biography

Matthew Flinders (1774–1814)

In 1802, the well-known British sea explorer Matthew Flinders set off from England on a very important journey. Flinders was the first person to sail around the entire Australian continent and carefully map its shores. The Great Barrier Reef posed big problems to ship captains. The sharp, rocky reefs could rip the bottom out of a wooden ship. After several attempts, Flinders succeeded in finding a safe passage through the reef. He spent 2 years exploring Australia. Today, this path is called Flinders Passage.

In 1814, Flinders's journals about this journey were published as a book titled *A Voyage to Terra Australis*. Coincidentally, Flinders died at the age of 40 on the very day his book was published.

Facts of Life

Born: 1774

Hometown: Donington, England

Occupation: Explorer, navigator

Died: 1814

The Big Picture

Coral reefs exist in many places around the world. They need shallow, warm water to support their complex ecosystem. This map shows some of the major coral reefs and the bodies of water that are their homes.

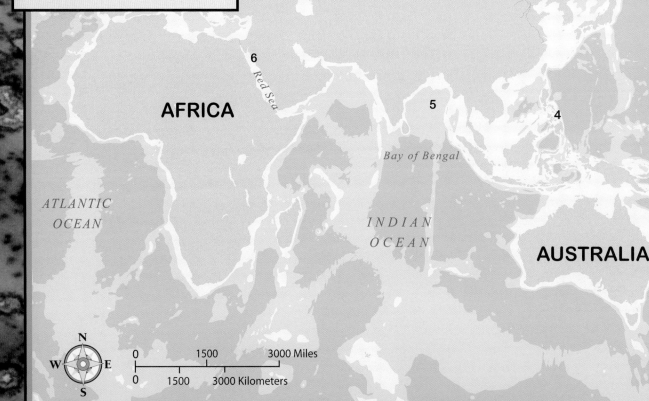

ARCTIC OCEAN

ASIA

EUROPE

6

Red Sea

AFRICA

5

4

Bay of Bengal

ATLANTIC OCEAN

INDIAN OCEAN

AUSTRALIA   3

N
W   E
S

0   1500   3000 Miles

0   1500   3000 Kilometers

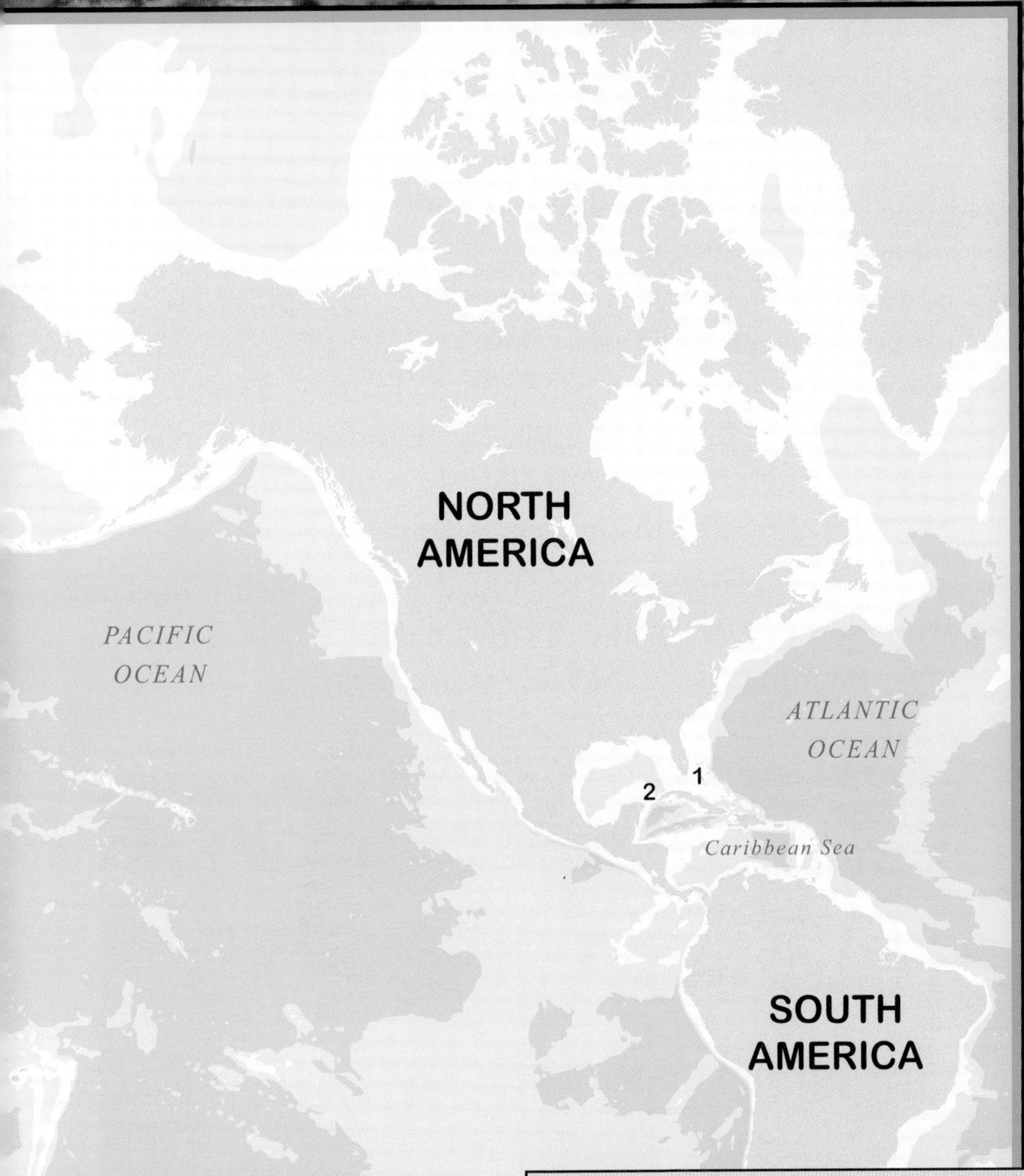

NORTH
AMERICA

*PACIFIC
OCEAN*

*ATLANTIC
OCEAN*

2   1

Caribbean Sea

SOUTH
AMERICA

*PACIFIC
OCEAN*

Reef Name or Location	Body of Water
1. Florida Keys	Atlantic Ocean
2. Mexico	Caribbean Sea
3. Australia	Pacific Ocean
4. Philippine Islands	Pacific Ocean
5. Indian Ocean Coral Reef	Indian Ocean
6. Red Sea Riviera Reefs	Red Sea

People of the Reef

Aboriginal Australians and Torres Strait Islanders lived in Australia for thousands of years before British explorers arrived. Aboriginal Australians lived in areas near the Great Barrier Reef, and Torres Strait Islanders lived on northern islands between Australia and Papua New Guinea. When Europeans began building colonies in Australia, many of these **indigenous** peoples were treated poorly, sometimes violently. As newcomers built more cities and towns, indigenous peoples were forced out of places where they had lived for generations. Eventually, Aboriginal Australians were forced to live in Australia's hot, dry, inland region called the Outback.

Today, indigenous Australian people have reclaimed some of their homelands. They are treated with more respect by the Australian government. They are involved in decisions about managing the reef environment.

One of Australia's main landmarks is Uluru, which stands on Aboriginal land.

Dugongs

Aboriginal Australians and Torres Strait Islanders believe nature is **sacred**. For instance, sea mammals called dugongs are very special creatures in these peoples' cultures. While dugongs are worshiped, they are also hunted for food.

The dugong is an **endangered** species. Overhunting could cause it to become extinct. The Australian government allows Aboriginal Australians to hunt a controlled number of dugongs. In return, the Aboriginal people work to protect the animals and ensure they will remain a part of the Great Barrier Reef forever.

Dugongs live off the Australian coast and in other areas of the Pacific and Indian Oceans.

Stories from the Reef

The earliest stories told in Australia were Aboriginal tales of "the dreaming" or "dreamtime." The dreaming explains many Aboriginal religious beliefs, such as how the world began. To this day, indigenous peoples tell and act out stories about the places in Australia they consider sacred, including the Great Barrier Reef.

When early English explorers visited Australia, they wrote adventure stories about the treacherous conditions in the country and the oceans surrounding it. Legends about terrifying sea creatures inspired French author Jules Verne to write *20,000 Leagues Under the Sea* in 1870. It is a thrilling novel that takes place partly in Australia.

The reef continues to enchant people today. In 2003, the animated film *Finding Nemo* brought the Great Barrier Reef to life on movie screens around the world.

■ This ancient rock painting tells part of an Aboriginal dreamtime story about fabled sea creatures.

Music in Nature

Aboriginal Australians invented some of the world's most unique instruments. One of the best-known Australian instruments is the didgeridoo. Originally, these long, hollow instruments were made from tree branches that had been hollowed out by termites. Today, most are made with tools by craftspeople.

The low sounds made when musicians blow through a didgeridoo imitate sounds in nature, such as running water, swaying trees, and thunder. Even some of Australia's pop and rock music groups use didgeridoo music.

■ **Didgeridoos are beautifully decorated for Aboriginal ceremonies.**

Natural Attractions

There are many things to see and do on a trip to the Great Barrier Reef. People from across Australia and the world visit this area to enjoy its natural beauty. Snorkeling and scuba diving are popular activities in the reef. People wear masks and special gear so they can spend a great deal of time underwater. Divers are advised to look at the underwater life, but not to touch. Many of the sea creatures are beautiful, but some can be dangerous to humans.

Visitors also love to fish in the reef area, but strict rules govern where and how people may fish. The Australian government makes every effort to ensure that human visitors do not damage the precious reef.

▄▄ Divers must be careful not to interfere with the reef ecosystem. Simply breaking off a piece of coral can destroy hundreds of years of growth.

Recipe

In Australia, the weather is almost always warm, so people eat outdoors on "barbies," or barbecues. Even restaurants serve food cooked on barbies, including vegetables, meat, fresh fish, and freshly caught seafood. Ask an adult to help you make this delicious Australian dish.

Australian Shrimp on the Barbie (serves 8)

$\frac{1}{2}$ cup (118 milliliters) melted butter

$\frac{1}{4}$ cup (59 ml) olive oil

mixed herbs (1 teaspoon each: thyme, parsley, and cilantro)

3 tablespoons fresh lemon juice

3 crushed garlic cloves

1 tablespoon chopped shallot

$1\frac{1}{2}$ pounds (680 grams) peeled shrimp

salt and pepper to taste

lemon wedges

Clean and peel the shrimp. Combine the butter, oil, herbs, lemon juice, garlic, and shallots in a large bowl. Mix in the shrimp and let sit in the refrigerator for 1 hour. Place the shrimp on skewers, and grill on medium heat until they are pink on both sides (about 2 minutes). Serve with lemon wedges.

Protecting the Reef

The Great Barrier Reef is one of the healthiest coral reefs in the world, but it must be protected to survive. Many of Australia's 19 million people live in or near coastline cities. Large numbers of people living and building cities in these areas create threats to the reef. Industries, such as construction, fishing, logging, and manufacturing, can add **pollution** to the air and water. Pollution can disrupt or destroy the reef ecosystem.

Individual people also can cause damage. Fishers who drop boat anchors sometimes break off large pieces of coral. Scuba divers can harm certain sea creatures by simply touching them. Even the activity of swimming can cause problems. Scientists believe that human sweat and suntan lotion washed off swimmers can disrupt the chemical balance in reef waters.

■ **Construction along Australia's western coast can damage the reef.**

The Australian government has passed laws limiting the areas where people can fish and dive. Much of the reef is a protected national park, so damaging the reef is illegal. The growth of human communities, however, is more difficult to control. What can the government do to stop towns and cities from expanding in one of the most beautiful spots on Earth?

Should the government restrict human activity on the Great Barrier Reef?	
YES	**NO**
Industries can cause pollution in reef waters.	The Australian coast is beautiful, and people want to experience the reef.
Fishing interferes with the ecosystem by taking certain animals out of the reef.	Fishing these waters brings a large amount of money into the national economy.
Scuba divers and other swimmers can disturb the ecosystem.	If people can scuba dive in the reef, they may become aware of its importance. They will be more likely to preserve the area.

Time Line

5–4 billion years ago
Earth forms.

600–300 million years ago
Seas rise and fall over
Earth's continents.

65 million years ago
Dinosaurs become extinct.

50 million years ago
Australia separates from
the other continents.

500,000 years ago
Land forms where the Great
Barrier Reef now sits.

50,000 years ago
Aboriginal Australians are
living in Australia.

10,000 years ago
The **Ice Age** ends, and water
levels rise.

8,000–6,000 years ago
The Great Barrier Reef begins
to form.

The orange-and-white
clown fish is one of more
than 500 species of fish
live in the Great Barrier F

Female sea turtles emerge from the
Great Barrier Reef waters once a year
to lay their eggs on the beach.

Cairns, Australia, is the largest city on the coast
of the Great Barrier Reef.

1400s
Chinese explorer Cheng Ho
(1371–1433) explores
Australia's north coast.

1642–1644
Dutch explorer Abel Tasman
(1603–1659) visits and maps
parts of Australia.

1770
James Cook claims Australia
for England.

Through centuries of growth and change, reefs often form spectacular shapes, such as coral arches.

1930s
The first hotel resorts are built on the Great Barrier Reef coast and islands.

1960s
Scientists become aware of crown-of-thorns starfish outbreaks, which damage large areas of coral.

1975
The Australian government establishes the Great Barrier Reef Marine Park, protecting the reef and its surrounding areas.

1981
The United Nations Educational, Scientific and Cultural Organization (UNESCO) names the Great Barrier Reef as a World Heritage Site.

1998
Warming sea temperatures cause massive coral bleaching in many worldwide coral reefs, including the Great Barrier Reef.

1788
England officially establishes the colony of New South Wales in Australia.

1801–03
Matthew Flinders explores and maps the Australian coast.

1901
Australia becomes a **commonwealth**.

What Have You Learned?

True or False?

Decide whether the following statements are true or false. If the statement is false, make it true.

1. About 1,000 species of animals live in the Great Barrier Reef.

2. The Great Barrier Reef is made up of many different reefs and coral islands, or cays.

3. Matthew Flinders was the first person to sail all the way around Australia.

4. Captain James Cook brought the first people to inhabit Australia.

5. Coral is a non-living thing.

6. The dugong is a endangered animal of the coral reef.

ANSWERS

1. False. About 10,000 species live in the Great Barrier Reef.

2. True

3. True

4. False. Aboriginal Australians and Torres Strait Islanders had been living there for thousands of years.

5. False. It is a living animal, but some kinds of corals turn to rock-like structures after they die.

6. True

Short Answer

Answer the following questions using
information from the book.

1. How many kinds of coral reef are there?

2. Who wrote *20,000 Leagues Under the Sea*?

3. How long have Aboriginal Australians lived
   in Australia?

4. What are the names of the world's major oceans?

5. How does building construction threaten a coral reef?

ANSWERS
1. Three: fringe, barrier, atoll
2. Jules Verne
3. More than 50,000 years
4. Pacific, Atlantic, Indian, Arctic
5. It can create pollution.

Multiple Choice

Choose the best answer for the
following questions.

1. Aboriginal Australians make
   didgeridoos from:
   a) paper
   b) tree branches
   c) coral

2. What animal can damage the
   coral reef?
   a) crown-of-thorns starfish
   b) soft coral
   c) whales

3. What are newly formed
   corals called?
   a) baby coral
   b) coral pups
   c) polyps

4. What happens during
   coral bleaching?
   a) coral dies
   b) coral is washed
   c) coral is born

ANSWERS
1. b
2. a
3. c
4. a

Find Out for Yourself

Books

Arnold, Caroline. *Uluru: Australia's Aboriginal Heart.* New York: Clarion Books, 2004.

Collard, Sneed B. *One Night in the Coral Sea.* Watertown, MA: Charlesbridge Publishing, 2005.

Doubilet, David. *Great Barrier Reef.* Washington, DC: National Geographic, 2002.

Web Sites

Use the Internet to find out more about the people, plants, animals, and geology of the Great Barrier Reef.

Great Barrier Reef Marine Park
www.gbrmpa.gov.au
This is the official site for the Australian government authority that oversees the reef.

ReefED
www.reefed.edu.au
This site provides educational information and activities on the Great Barrier Reef's ecosystems.

Reef Education Network
www.reef.edu.au
This site gives information on the environmental issues affecting the Great Barrier Reef.

Skill Matching Page

What did you learn? Look at the questions in the "Skills" column. Compare them to the page number of the answers in the "Page" column. Refresh your memory by reading the "Answer" column below.

SKILLS	ANSWER	PAGE
What facts did I learn from this book?	I learned that the Great Barrier Reef is the largest coral reef in the world.	4
What skills did I learn?	I learned how to read a map.	5, 7, 16–17
What activities did I do?	I answered the questions in the quiz.	28–29
How can I find out more?	I can read the books and visit the Web sites from the Find Out for Yourself section.	30
How can I get involved?	I can be careful not to disturb nature when swimming or scuba diving.	24

Glossary

Aboriginal Australians: the first peoples to live in Australia

algae: simple living things; tiny plant life that has no roots or flowers

bacteria: tiny living cells that cannot be seen without a microscope

commonwealth: a country or state governed by the people who live there, rather than by a king or queen

ecosystem: a group of living plants, animals, and their environment, all of which act as a community

endangered: threatened; nearly extinct

Ice Age: a period in Earth's history when huge glaciers covered large parts of the planet

indigenous: native to a certain place; having been born in a place

migrate: to move from one place to another

pollution: materials, such as waste or chemicals, that can harm the air, water, or land

polyps: small, tube-shaped sea creatures with tentacles for catching food

predator: an animal that hunts and kills other animals for food

sacred: spiritual, religious, and holy

species: a specific group of plant or animal that shares characteristics

Index